821
TRÉ

The Phoenix Living Poets

———————

THE SWANS OF BERWICK

The Phoenix Living Poets

THE SWANS OF
BERWICK

by

SYDNEY TREMAYNE

CHATTO AND WINDUS

THE HOGARTH PRESS

1962

562613

Published by
Chatto and Windus Ltd
with The Hogarth Press Ltd
42 William IV Street
London WC2

★

Clarke, Irwin and Co Ltd
Toronto

Acknowledgments

Acknowledgment is made to the editors of *The Listener*, *The Saltire Review*, *The Dubliner*, *New Poems 1957* (Michael Joseph), *New Poems 1961* (Hutchinson), *Best Poems of 1956* (U.S.A.), *Honour'd Shade*: an anthology of new Scottish poetry to mark the bicentenary of the birth of Robert Burns, *The Poetry Review*, *Poetry and Audience*, *The Yorkshire Post* and *Outposts*, in which some of these poems have appeared. The whole of this collection is recent work, with the one exception of *Drowned*, which was published originally in 1951.

821
TRE

Contents

Snow

Snow bends the branches of the wood.
Dust sheets are on the gorse. Still as a house
Long muffled up and left to emptiness,
The landscape dozes in a haze of cold.
Snow is heaped over bramble. All this land
Is planed and domed and sifted by the wind.
Trust it; enter it; never turn your head.

Only Music can Come Near

Who are you whom I address
With the silence of a thought?
Should I guess, it is no use.
All I know is, you are not
Goddess or public meeting, or
Some private pronoun singular,
Not a mirror, nor a face,
Nor entirely emptiness.

For wretchedness, for loneliness,
To that wall without an ear
Trusting prisoners confess
All the life they must immure,
And lovers, too, for joy will sing
To any safe, insentient thing,
More to cover than express
Their unprotected happiness.

I carved an icon in the wall,
A perjury, not life but death.
(Whoever can his true love tell,
Be wiser still, and hold his breath.)
All's farewell. No doubting this:
Silence best can silence kiss,
Yet the child talks to a doll.
Solitude invents the soul.

Balance may be, not control:
Usual winds of chaos cry.
Desire is endless, it is all,
All that our poems have to say.
To make a calm live on in air
Only music can come near,
As all confusions of the will
Love reconciles, and ever shall.

Time past, the tempest's fugitive,
I heard a rumour of no peace,
Of mortal love, how it must leave
And walk the world without a house.
Of time it's made, of time it makes
Image on image, which it breaks,
Since no pathos can survive.
This desire is all to save.

Yet no harmony can live
Except some dialogue agrees.
I hear a dead man's music move
Towards an image, but there is
No image, only the response,
At the last reach of utterance
Creative silence come alive,
Echoing in the empty cave.

The Still Hawk in the Air

I

It was the sun that hid the sea
Striking it like a sheet of tin.
It was the sun that nailed it firmly down
So you could walk upon it, like a fly
Walking on its reflection in a glass.
The sun put everything in place
Under the sun and in the shifty sky:
Either way up, a masterpiece
For Adam's bloodless joy.
Sun even beat his heart to save his breath,
A life with the advantages of death.

II

A weasel came down from my thatch
Dragging a young rat larger than itself
And set off on the flat, head lifted high,
Swaying from foot to foot for leverage.
The rat, fawn underside displayed,
And useless, delicate feet gone slack,
Went bumping across the frosted grass
Half on its back, half twisted to one side.
The weasel's joy was underscored in red:
Light swaggered in the small quick brain
That didn't know how vulnerable it was.
It stayed unsafe a moment in the sun,
Strutting to darkness near a beech tree's root.

Startling as blood on snow,
Impermanent as snow or blood,
Across enduring solitude
The trails of Adam go
Whose half made cities half decay,
Whose mind is scattered like a crowd,
Whose heart, defenceless as an eye,
Must unify
On peril of its life
Images that bring to grief
All pride of intellect, that wingless fly.

The still hawk in the air,
Steady as on a stair,
Stopped in mid-motion by an act of will,
Does not control its element
But on its prey intent
Strikes balance, countering chaos with a style.
Such harmony of opposites there:
Gauging reality, a force of air,
The purpose not to hover, but to kill.

Remembering in the night
The hawk's extravagant flight,
How wide it wheeled to aim so narrowly,
I hear the owls at work,
Slick hunters of the dark
Whose voices put the sun a world away;
But still no image comes to pacify
That sense persisting like a good
To which no argument can lead,
That shaken, half experienced harmony
Scouted by peaceful Caesar's discipline,
Such carefully inflicted pain.
The heart's a weasel for vitality;
There is no peace till world is left for dead.
Night, changing by an imperceptible shade,
Foretells the climbing sky, the hawk outspread.

One Morning

Learn that this almost visionary place
Was simply home: the sound is not distress,
The sound of morning flying with the wind
Across the white sea and the sparkling land.
The sea vibrating through the naked beach,
The mesmerising sea, that with a pitch
Shoots thinly to my feet, has wasted out
Wastes that obsessed me once but here do not:
My family's finish, my own change, the whole
Longwinded wandering story since the Fall.
Instead my heart is lifted on the light
Out of the episodes of time in flight,
As if the burning bush I may not face
Made this original daylight that gulls cross,
Lending a shape and body to the air.
There is no time to wonder or to care,
While this luck holds, what permanence is here,
What core of constancy or truce to war.
I am expressed by things, and what responds
Is of those things, ungrieving as the winds,
As though the revelation should be this
Reflection upon spirit in its place
Of light reflected also by the stones.
Nothing of this is mine, or anyone's.
The beauty of the morning that begins
When I am words on paper has no signs
Of being entered or departed from.

Against the sky the seabirds flash, or dim
Into the distance. Further seabirds come,
Uttered like grace notes round a stronger theme:
The solitude is full of solitudes
Searching on wings the high, invisible roads,
The indivisible roads that do not meet
In distance dancing, or in space alight.

This Common Ground

The light turned out, going up to bed, I stop,
Held by the sudden outline of the trees,
The shape the hedge gives to the sky, the drop
Outward through darkness to the lamps that blaze
Far off along the road edge of the night.
The land comes in upon me like a song,
Freshly familiar, and the sense of height
That is returning joy foiled by no wrong.
I stand in darkness, know my way in it,
Touch-in the unseen fields and the near wood.
The placed sense entering that the light kept out
Identifies all that through time withstood
The rationalising world's waste paper rage.
We live by our affections: where they grow
No prying mind will catch them in a cage;
These are our silences, telltale or no.
You are asleep whose ghost and mine may share
This common ground that seems like solitude
Only because our grasp is light as air,
And cut no name into the moss-green wood.

Familiar Solitude

I have been one who worked at night
And left the light and entered the cold street
And looked up at the stars burning to waste,
Hard stars, and the great city, freed from haste,
Riding beneath them on the dark,
Its drudges absent, judges, men of mark
All buried in oblivion centuries deep
Since nightfall, since the darkness opened up
The spaciousness and desert scale of night.
I have heard silence strengthened out
By the low argument of tide and Thames,
And pauses in the wind like dying flames
Even when war lit bonfires in the streets.
Quietness flowed then over shouts
Of struggling men as water flows round stones
Or life moves dark and brilliant through the veins.
Slow as the tide, the undersound
Of those long hours in which pretensions end.
These fingers find the key by years of use,
Familiar solitude a living-place.

Ring Cycle

Aye, when delight was the assured response,
Then in the earth no meaningful dead thing
Distrained upon the heart; days were at once
Lucky in love and empty as a ring
That, held up, frames a world in light.
The ring upon a finger clasped a life
In all its dark and promise and its fright.
The ring left on a bone – that's for the thief
To lift up to the light and see it shine
And claim his new love set in such a frame
Most beautiful on earth. The same design
Must be observed in every coupling game:
Meeting is world's beginning, so intense
No dead have lived, there is no word for time.
Bury delight, since guards fail in defence,
Shallow delight that had a tinkling chime
When love could run, that now must stand and care
For what the earth has eaten. All's transformed
Into this empty shining of the air,
Wakeful intensity, the defence disarmed.

The Swans of Berwick

Swans, like a yacht race in a heavy sea,
Scudding for Berwick under a dark sky,
Come like creation, wake the world alive,
Confer malevolence on the dead wave,
Storm into harbour in a tight array.

Sealed in a senseless cold of troubled mind,
A split-off deadness, deadness walking round,
I, greyness locked in absence, saw them come
Sudden as joy to focus present time,
And was awake and trod on real ground.

Life in foreboding cities drowns in talk.
The mind pulled from its senses hides to seek
The clear sight that it had, an active sight:
No sharper sight than this, no deeper night
Than dead wits walking where the dead seas quake.

Out of the mists of Berwick drive the swans,
Great, powerful birds intent on wild concerns
And making haste before the rising squall.
The slicing waves roll over the sea wall.
The swans plunge through; the cloud follows and rains.

Wind Shakes the House

Again it moves, that millrace sweep of air;
Gales wrench the trees, a deep, continuous roar
Floods through the dark, and ebbs, and flings again
Wind of a solid force and thudding rain.
Half in, half out, my sheltered senses fly.
Drowning in air I filled my lungs to cry
My first breath back on such a night of noise,
Then through a month of storms that tore up trees
I slept, woke, slept, knowing neither world nor me,
Nursed in the void preceding memory's eye.
Tonight is like recovering by ear
Rhythm of breathing, as the wind draws near
In a long gust that rakes from the world's end
And shakes the house, making the windows bend
To which involuntarily I look to see
Some speck, some print that is not washed away
But catch instead my own face, two wars old.
Put out the light: the blinded spirit's pulled
Into the darkness where it cannot live.
Black chaos bound together like a wave
Slides without breaking over freezing space.
Enter the rage within the body's house,
Warm, squalling brat. The storm beats at the door
(Waves in a shell), the house yours to explore:
Its twisting corridors, its whispering stairs,
Junk, dust, and damp, and unidentified smears.

Arrival in Edinburgh

The leaves blow, and the rain whips Princes Street.
Crowds are unchanged; they with bent heads go by
And leaves blow and the grey lid of the sky
Comes down and shuts me in, and as I wait
My mind, spooled out along the Great North Road,
Slowly retracts itself into this place.
Across two decades of forgetfulness
By memory of the senses I am led.
It was my parents' city. They are dead,
Dead for so long I shall not look to meet
Donald or Isabel, Doreen, Hector, Kate,
Margaret, Evelyn, Arthur, Winifred;
All have grown fictional, and thus complete,
While, in suspense, breathing the lively air,
I step for the first time unguarded here.
Under the rain, the city, sponged like slate,
Rooted as racial memory, dark and raw,
Resumes me like a dogma; subtle wynds
Lead me through tenements whose bulk withstands
Great winds, if not the little doubts that gnaw.
Some shock of the familiar is forced in:
Over the glistening stones, as if the sea
Hardened and held me up, I feel my way,
Listening to my own footsteps, and the rain,
And voices gossiping on stairs, and wheels
Rumbling on granite setts. Each common phrase
Of this domestic city slowly grows
Into its place, as durable as the walls,
And I climb up, as usual, to look out,
Searching this drama of the high and low,
This town that gives an edge to the stone sky,
To catch the whole scene in the plainest light.

Surely I live this twice, or superimpose
One image upon the other with no join:
It is as though, this instant, child and man
Breathed the one breath and held with neutral eyes
That slating wind, the grey and forceful wind
Stretching the smoke out in long, active lines.
This pattern upon the air, of strenuous reins,
Locates the prevailing sky, time out of mind,
Which is not home for anything, even a bird.
At soaring distance, in a blustering space
Where no face interposes and no voice
Calls for an answer, or intrudes a word,
The mind, released into its solitude,
Breaking involvement in the muddle and stress,
Deceives itself perhaps, for it would bless
Even the sense of time, that sense here made
From roofs and swollen hills and the great sky,
The unknown living and unpossessive dead,
And journeys past in many a tangled wood,
And ignorance beyond hope to clarify.
So I come down. The landmarks keep the place.
The crowds flow round them, and the traffic's noise.
The castle, built on a volcano, shows
The endearing irony of the human case,
This fort that a single hit would vaporise.
The quarrelling parents, nowhere reconciled,
Were young here and were happy. I unfold
All I remember, all I can compose,
Like a torn map whose holes let through some light.
I join the crowd, my step fits with the crowd,
I go surrounded in a solitude
Where crowds flow and the rain whips Princes Street.

The Galloway Shore

Sand white as frost: the moon stayed hard and high.
Far off, the lights around the Irish coast
Leapt up like salmon. An Iscariot sea
Chinked on the rocks. Within a shadow cast
By broken cliffs, a place of slippery stones,
I faced the speaking lights, small human signs
Of hidden rocks and granite patiences.
Among the sounds of night a slithering wind,
Darkness on dark, in fitful cadences
Phrased the fresh world. There is no older sound.

Never was stillness here, where I began
To watch alone, to be an emptiness,
To let the strongly running world come in
As seldom can be done: this was to pass
Into no trance but a most brilliant waking,
Active as light upon the deep tide snaking
Before my sight, so lately lost in crowds.
The force that moves all things and lives me out
Made me its filament; all that divides
Time into stints could be no longer thought.

To be had no past tense: all sense was new.
There was destruction of irrelevance.
A listener to the world, I heard it flow
So huge, so slow, it seemed like permanence
Experienced for an eye-blink. Darting knives
Made slits of light. My years, those forty thieves
Crowded together in one brimming jar,
Left me no wish to grieve for. All this hoard
Was poured out in an instant to the air,
While I was bankrupt even of a word.

Was it some trick to steal the peace of the dead?
It was not peace but power, surely the source
Of every light lit in a transient head
From Genesis to Einstein. In this place
(Austere, coherent, callous) all deeds done,
Bastilles of knowledge, crumpled. The moon's lane,
Quickened with silver, ran; all near was dark,
The land behind most dark. Spread round the sea,
Pinpricks of light timed out a few men's work,
Wakeful in cells impenetrable by me.

Our time seeks for an idol. There is none.
The image that you want is not a city,
Nothing so pitiable; the sea pours in
And shears your dwellings down, ignores your duty
To house a purpose, bears you to extreme.
The lights were warning lights by which I came
As polar travellers come to what is real
In all their banished days. The sight was calm.
There is not any will, or wall, or cell
Would keep this calmness out. Give it no name.

Growing, the poem's dumb, planted in change
Immeasurable and ineluctible.
It flowers in light. We reach outside our range
Into the sureness, indestructible,
That sings us out of time. Whose is our voice?
It is the voice of stones that waste, of seas
That cannot rest, of air transfixed by light:
That is to say a human voice, that tries,
Always in solitude, aided by night,
To be identified with all of these.

The sun's white shadow darkened all the sea
With cool and bearable light. I knew this dark;
It was the earth between me and the day
And this my turning place, a boundary mark.
The brittle sea fractured along the coast.
The Irish lights jigged on, fixed points that placed
My world on stone foundations. They put space
A little farther off where men marooned
In granite kept their watch. The moon was glass.
I leaned against a rock, out of the wind.

Remote Country

The way goes snaking upward through the heat.
Out of the carving river's narrow space
Shaken with noise of water, black and white,
You climb at last into a scooped out place
Where nothing moves but wind treading the grass.

All cover's past. Below, the waterfalls
Dig out of sight, like memory. You stare up,
Strange in this trap ringed all about by hills,
To find the one way out, confined and steep,
Watched by whatever eyes look from the top.

When you have crossed the open, reached the height,
It is a brown plateau, cratered and bare,
Low, lumpy hills and black, eroded peat
Stretching as far as light can throw its glare,
No living thing in sight in sky or moor.

Mind finds its way to meet with solitude.
Bear this in mind: the image will not age
Of desert, light and always moving cloud.
It is a vision to exhaust all rage.
Calculate nothing. Leave an empty page.

The Estuary

When you have climbed so far in loneliness,
The river, Arnold's image, flowing light,
Seen from a height is coiled, continuous light.
From estuary to source it lies remote
Linking its hills and woodland, factories, wharves,
River and eye receptacles for light.
Between low mudbanks crusted with white birds
The river broadens out: flatness and space,
And one barge anchored, solid. But for that
You might be drowned in sky. All ways are sky
Beyond the brown marsh in the broad sea light.
When was there ever blindness bright as this?
None but the shallow pool of the clear stones.
There even now the light must float its chevrons
Like the reflections of migrating geese.

Endings

Endings may prove perplexing shifts to make,
Beginnings trick by slamming doors.
In the stripped house the start was to forsake.
Resounding were the emptied floors.
Tread tiptoe or the noise outpaced comes back
That has been deadened safely by the years.

The ticking of a watch filled the whole place.
In the stilled street the night air peeled
The rigid mask from the young, heated face.
I see now, when the truth is cold,
The wish to go pulled back against release.
From broken gaols some wait to be expelled.

Beneath spent time, where there is no suspense,
The dusty wooden puppets lie,
Once pulled together by the strings of chance.
A villain of the deepest dye
Destroys conviction by his comic stance.
Novel interpretations multiply.

To go round with the earth brings light to bear.
In one day's revolution, all
The serviceable hatreds having power
To prop the king and rule the fool
May crumble: like a wall that isn't there
When reached for, the surprise is not to feel.

An old man, country neighbour, lies now dead.
This was the scene where he was born.
He lived here eighty years and called life good,
Or fair, except that it was worn.
For sixty years a craftsman working wood,
He died as whiteness opened on the thorn.

And now his sons come hurrying to the house
And mount the stairs to the known room.
Outside, a rattling milk van breaks the peace,
The birds sing loud, the day is calm.
This ending was not complex but precise,
Full stop to sleep and sleep's half surfaced dream.

The root is dead that never came to light.
The tree throughout its length is dead.
One man is dead, his eighty years unsplit.
Turncoat emotions pick their side.
Living, no change is done with, none so neat.
Sleep tricked the wish to stay out of its stride.

Slow Spring

A bitter wind cuts down the daffodils.
The yellow sun goes down after the gales.
Smaller than match heads are the buds on thorns.
They will not flare before the weather turns.

One twig of blossom on a half dead tree.
One peewit dives and swerves with his spring cry.
One old man in his cottage, living alone,
Looks out, stays in. Another day is gone.

Bomb Incident

Upon a yellow night
Cinders were falling through the air.
We, lacking means to fight
The flowering spread of fire,
Watched from the street the swell department store
Shake out its wings of gold, resigned to soar
Past profit into loss,
Winning uncalculated grace
While follies by the gross
Went up in heaven's face.
Night hid a holy ragamuffin smile:
Uprush of angels issued from the pile
As down the pillars fell.
We were a grimy band, and few.
We could not hope to tell
How generous and new
The prospect seemed, clear swept by accident.
That was our folly, a past incident.

Black and White

This wintry day
I watched the sun
Within a few hours run
Its light away.

Time is short, short
For reaching through
Into the distant view;
Ages depart

With no found sight.
Vision goes waste;
World closes; darkly mist
Overflows night.

My window's black.
Like polished stone
It seems to shut light in,
Give shadows back.

Between tight lines
A shine of glass
Frames clock face, human face;
Beyond begins,

Begins in doubt,
A shade of white:
A ragged rose, too late,
Freshly come out.

To grow so far
But end in frost,
Is all that labour lost?
There's power to spare:

Crammed summers blast
Out of the dust.
This rose, because it must,
Makes room at last.

Winter was bare.
A shade of white
Contrasting with the night
Becomes a flare.

Moses

Head in a cloud Moses stands
Beckoning with explosive hands,
Threatening unpromised lands.

Tutmouse the Pharaoh rather bored
Hears the wind harp through his beard.
His heart is hardened by the Lord.

Superior persons tend to miss
Unreasoning people's deadliness.
Pharaoh is sunk because of this.

Pillar of cloud, pillar of fire,
Songs and timbrels fill the air.
Logic never led so far.

Moses harder than a stone
With the Laws engraved thereon
Knocks the gods and Pharaoh down.

In the desert, furious,
Rules with God's and Pharaoh's voice,
For the chosen have no choice.

The Ides of March

Security and certainty:
How the human race does cry
For its angell infancy.
Have you not heard Vesuvius roar
Underneath the nursery floor?
Or observed the pearly tear
Dissolve and leave the vinegar?
Where the tyrant lays his head
Stand no angels round the bed.
The stars are far. They influence
No change in human circumstance.
I watch the stars. My mind is still:
Not for Caesar will these fall.
I watch the moon I cannot have
White as Caesar in his grave.

The Hilltop House

Learning to be at home upon this hill
In a lone house surrounded by the sky,
My mind, as if compelled to justify
Each moment of its time, could not be still.
It was disturbed by so much altering light;
Sun, stars and seasons gathered speed
Whirling like leaves around my head
That tried to hold too much of day and night.

It is the laziest fallacy of all
To think that in the country time runs slow.
See it advance in all live things that grow;
Suspect it when it sleeps, a faultless wheel
Shining because of speed 'from sky to sky'.
What foolishness for mind to chase
That which encircles it, and race
The spinning brightness that excites the eye.

The presence of the past in all I see
Brings distant summers in when summer's gone.
The mind has this advantage, to move on
And yet to dim no daylight quality.
Light on wet leaves, the trees are waterfalls:
That image for the leaves that shake
Gleams against blackness of a rock
Far off in time: I hear its rumbling pools.

Where I was born beside the curling sea
Waking, or dropping off to sleep, I'd hear
The rushing sky, autumn's familiar roar,
Time on my side, glad for the wind to blow
And drive the fears of silent dark away.
The rushing sky, the neutral wind
Span the landscapes of the mind
Where I draw breath, committed mortally.

Living exposed to every weather's force,
Having to beat through all the gales that lash
This hilltop, noisy as a naked bush,
My shelter frail, my choice, to some, perverse,
I see the fiery beech of fifteen boles
Rooted in doubleness of light,
And in the blindness of the night
Wake to the far sound where the grey sea rolls.

Journey in One Place

The rain goes on and on. The ground is sodden.
Day after day the valley's depth is hidden.
The hill ends in pale cloud that isn't sky
But flat, continuous emptiness, a grey
Beyond which there's no shape, and sense turns back.
It is a season soft as a straw stack,
The lane mashed mud, the bracken soaked to rust.
Stray gusts, ghosts made of mist, go bulging past
The stripped woods and the thorns hung with clear beads.
Trees shake themselves like dogs, flinging cascades
Of raindrops noisily on littered leaves.
Be ready for our journey: the time moves.
Soon we must traverse the blank days of snow
In which the tracks of birds are all that show,
When icicles, those straight transparent horns,
Glitter, implausible as unicorns,
With sharp east light that breaks off in the hand.
When we have stared across the silent land
And watched the loaded sun, dull red and large,
Reflect along the snowfield like a forge,
Our room will be an island in the night,
Lighthouse for owls, most curiously bright.

Smooth Landscape

The long, low hills, the sky, the little fields:
A boneless country founded on no rock,
A moulded country offering no holds
To take the eyes up slowly. Without check
The eye sweeps over it along the sky
And almost naturally is taught to fly.

Smooth landscape, filled as much with flint as flowers,
Opened by sunlight, narrowed by the rain,
Those who have learned how brilliance disappears
Wait best for change to bring it back again
Out of the mist that settles in for days,
Consumes the sky and makes a smoke of trees.

Friends

He talks compulsively. I feel
His words like ash falling from coal.
He talks not to communicate
But to unpick some rankling knot.
The coil is snagged around my brain,
A ligature of, almost, pain.
An incident fished from his youth
Swims with a barb struck through his mouth.
I'm audience. He has this claim
For often I have talked the same.
Now he is lightened of some ghost
While I am heavy and oppressed.
To let this pass, I walk alone
Where grass is whitened by the moon.
Here, where dark trees open out,
Is silence, and a little light.

The Fox

A vision of silence startled me:
A sinuous fox lightfooting past my door.
Out of the corner of his yellow eye
Glanced round his shoulder. Seeing nothing there,
Skirted the tall dry biscuit coloured grass
Unhurriedly, choosing the open way;
Like an hallucination passed across
To spring the trap forgotten many a day.

One who was brave and frightened, fugitive,
Fox coloured hair, eyes full of level flames,
Leaps out of buried memory to live,
The brightest thing in daylight. Swiftly comes
The verbal thought how many years she's dead.
The fox has slipped away in the dense wood.

Two Hacks

The valley emerging from a shining mist.
Black, but not solid black, treetops appear.
The hillcrest opposite, out of the cloud
Floats like an island, holding up a spire.

I know, if I went down into the mist,
Then climbed up through the fields, sliding in mire,
To the botched village and that flinty church,
I'd hear some worthy man hold forth in there.

Therefore I don't. The morning, still as paint,
Surrounds me like my youth, and I could dare
Set free the word of beauty that's locked up,
Saved for advertisements of women's wear.

Alas, I have a duty piece to write
On politics and worthy men whose care
Is for the public good and governance
And peace, and honour, and the party war.

Lovers

After the drought that cracked the land across
There came a flood, and bubbling through the ground
Extended to a lake all round the house
So that when night came, clear and with no wind,
Stars and the passing lights of aeroplanes
Caught in this steady lake unrolled the sky
In place of vanished flower beds and lost lawns.
The house became an ark to float or fly
Between two skies, far from the anchored earth
Whence the planes came and whither they went back,
Not seeking us; from us no dove went forth
Who in each other's arms until daybreak
Would not bear space between us, but compressed
Two firmaments in lightning's single star.
Surprised at morning: earth lay fresh and moist,
Our well-starred moat vanished within the hour.

Space Travel

A place comes into mind, and I breathe there.
I see a white bull among yellow flags
Cropping the grass; the sun is hot, the air
Broods, and a ledge of road zigzags
Steeply above the loch. The olive hills
In the unwrinkling tidal water keep
The blue sky off the shore. A burn that spills
Down from the treeless moor of deer and sheep
Fills out the stillness with a steady sound.
My fingers feel the grained stone of a wall,
The scent of heat comes from the peaty ground
And scent of bracken standing dense and tall.
Place into mind, or mind into this place,
It is time bodily lifted off its track
For no cause that I know. Nothing can pace
Such time as this. It is not calling back
Minutely into memory where we've been;
It is a lived experience, sharpening change,
Hours stretching out whose presence lies between
Two sentences; there like a mountain range.
Minds cannot share their places. Even in bed
And in the dark, in closest harmony
Where we lie stitching time with double thread,
We might as well be stitching up the sea
As think our visions run through the same eye.
Where have you been? I did not see you go.
I was beyond the mountains where the sky
Looks different. You did not even know.

Explosive Dust

What is done is done, is done
Shouts the starling in the sun.
Belsen's buried in the brain.
Roots that thirst like weasels rip
Earth and what earth covers up.
Every crime and more to come
Is the promise of each time
Yet the world outlives the lot.
Generations are on heat:
In shining ignorance like flame
The newest creatures, without blame,
Rise in vigour of their blood
To stalk each other through the wood.
Constantly the world disowns
Canting sermons upon stones
And consumes its rotten bones.
Mind draws nothing, the sun must,
From the past's explosive dust.

Old Poems

These distant selves, more pleasant than I am,
Though I can see their maladroitness plainly,
They leave some brightness. They remind me mainly
Of plowtering through a bog, and then a climb,
Flushed with excitement though a trifle wheezy,
Towards the great top note like a red plum
There on the wildest peak of Christendom
For those whose hearts are strong and spirits breezy.

It seems we lose some good for a hard gain,
Loss by evaporation probably
Since we're reduced now to economy
And keeping powder dry, while on our skin,
No longer like a plum but racked boot leather,
Poems of truth are written by the weather.
Clearly, we are the book and not the pen;
The truth is in us. We can't read it either.

A Country Lawyer

A stuttering solicitor
Exploding through his whiskers:
Such was this ancient bachelor,
None of your dapper friskers.

He wore the Samson of moustaches,
Ragged, and drooping like a sporran.
It served to muffle verbal flashes
Which thereby gained, as wit that's foreign.

His spectacles were densely pebbled
And hid the light that shone behind them;
If Benches got his words unravelled
Science was in his specs to blind them.

His hair resembled argument,
Being a long and dusty tangle,
His coat stained like a monument
Where flocks of starlings roost and wrangle.

The convolutions of his trousers
Possessed their personal incoherence.
Few in the bookshop tribe of browsers
Achieve more derelict appearance.

These signs ensured from circuit judges
Exceptional and courteous patience,
The English way that seldom grudges
Politeness shown to poor relations.

His clients, wise in country fashion,
Were not misled by such externals:
Hard nuts not anxious for compression
Such as might bring the court to kernels.

O master of incompetence,
O virtuoso of confusion,
One who could tangle evidence
Until a fact would be intrusion,

That I should write your epitaph
Is cause in me of true dejection.
I add 'Lie still', and if you laugh
Grass whiskers shield you from detection.

Live Owl, Dead Poets

In spring the cat-voiced little owl
That nests in our beech tree
Is moved all night to yip and yowl
Requiring company.

Urgent and feminine that voice.
It claws awake the night,
Making the poems run like mice
To hide themselves from sight.

Often a run of thought is lost
Through listening to that bird,
And well I see why thought's a ghost
When lusting life is heard.

Last night on Margaret's gramophone
We heard the poets read.
Silent we sat while thought was drawn
Like razor across thread.

Dead men turning in their grooves
Who could not hear a sound;
Vibrations echoing out of loves
Switched off, gone underground:

Over and over we compared
The well-wrought patterns played.
The intimate performance starred
The strangers who were dead.

O let the little screech owl screech
That startles night alive.
Welcome a screech owl in our beech
While both of us survive.

47

Roots

At this point where I now am,
Like weed that floats,
I who should be a rooted man
Put down my roots.
Air yields a bit, and water
Makes me a place;
Here, as a link in movement,
Let it be by choice,
Since choice is a weighty matter
And man needs weight,
Paying down root like a plummet
To keep up straight.

Drowned

I am dissolved and laid upon the wind;
The sun darts through me, diving with the terns
That strike the sea and with the light rebound.
I am rounded to the stillness of the stones
On which gulls perch in shallows where the hulls
Of painted boats are flickering with the light,
A jiggling light of white and coloured shells.
I am smoothed across the sky and I forget
What name I had, what purport, what desire,
Being other than the name was, being transformed
Into the elements of all desire.
The light sleeps on my village that is farmed
Down to the sand in strips of green and gold
Where nets spread to the sun dry brown as hair.
The folk have all gone to the harvest field;
The blue loch left alone, it is quiet here.